SALES

Steps to Success

Effective Steps for Navigating a New Career in Sales

Eric S. Campbell

Copyright © 2024 by Eric S. Campbell

All rights reserved. No part of this publication may be reproduced, distributed, or transmitted in any form or by any means, including photocopying, recording, or other electronic or mechanical methods, without the prior written permission of the publisher, except in the case of brief quotations embodied in critical reviews and certain other noncommercial uses permitted by copyright law.

"Hello, I'm Eric Campbell, a seasoned retail professional with over two decades of experience in delivering exceptional customer service. My journey in sales began in 2001, taking an unexpected turn from my initial career in mental health. After a leadership stint with my father-in-law's company, I transitioned into retail, where I honed my skills in building genuine relationships with customers. My philosophy is simple: serve, don't sell. As I always say, 'Customers don't care how much you know until they know how much you care.' In this 10-step sales process, I'll share my expertise on how to prioritize your customers' needs, establish trust, and create a personalized experience that sets you apart from the rest."

Table of Contents

Page Left Blank Intentionally

Chapter One: Prospecting

Prospecting is the first and most crucial step in the sales process. It involves identifying potential customers (prospects) and researching their needs to tailor your approach effectively. This foundational step sets the stage for a successful sales journey by building a robust pipeline of qualified leads.

Prospecting is the first step in the sales process. It involves identifying potential customers and researching their needs. This step is critical because it sets the stage for the rest of the sales process.

Examples of prospecting include:

- Research companies and industries to identify potential customers
- Using social media to connect with potential customers
- Attending networking events to meet potential customers
- Using sales intelligence tools to find contact information and company data
- Some examples of prospecting in action include:
- A salesperson researching companies in a specific industry and creating a list of potential customers
- A salesperson using LinkedIn to connect with decision-makers at potential customer companies
- A salesperson attending a trade show and collecting business cards from potential customers
- Identify potential customers through research, social media, and networking events
- Create a list of target companies and decision-makers

- Use sales intelligence tools to gather information about potential customers

Here's an example of step 1, Prospecting:

Let's say you're a salesperson for a company that sells marketing automation software and looking to prospect for new customers.

You start by researching companies that fit your ideal customer profile (ICP). Your ICP includes companies that:

- Are in the healthcare industry
- Have a marketing team of at least five people
- Use a CRM system
- Have an annual revenue of at least $10 million

You use LinkedIn Sales Navigator to search for companies that fit your ICP. You identify 20 companies that match your criteria and list their contact information.

Next, you use a sales intelligence tool to gather more information about each company, such as their current marketing technology stack, company news, and key decision-makers.

You then use this information to personalize your outreach emails and phone calls to each company. For example, you might write an email like this:

"Hi [Decision-Maker's Name],

I came across [Company Name] and noticed you're using [current marketing technology]. I wanted to reach out and introduce you to our marketing automation software, which can help you streamline your marketing processes and improve efficiency.

Would you be open to a quick call to discuss further?

Best,

[Your Name]"

This is just one example of how you might prospect for new customers. The key is to identify companies that fit your ICP and then use personalized outreach to grab their attention.

Here are some other ways you might prospect for new customers:

- Use social media to connect with potential customers and build relationships
- Attend industry events and conferences to network with potential customers
- Use sales intelligence tools to gather information about potential customers and identify potential pain points
- Use email marketing campaigns to reach out to potential customers and promote your product or service

Remember, prospecting is about finding and qualifying potential customers, so research and personalize your outreach to increase your chances of success!

Personal Reflection: Overcoming the Prospecting Challenge – As someone who grew up as a friendly but shy child, I often shied away from situations that could lead to rejection. The idea of prospecting, with its inherent risk of rejection, felt daunting. However, as I built confidence in myself and gained a deep understanding of the value of what I was selling, my perspective changed. I realized that sharing the benefits of our product was not just a sales tactic but a way to genuinely help others. This shift in mindset allowed me to embrace prospecting with enthusiasm and commitment, transforming it from a source of anxiety into an exciting opportunity to connect and offer value.

Key Concepts in Prospecting

Strategies for Identifying and Qualifying Potential Customers

- **Cold Calling:** Reaching out to potential customers who have had no prior contact with your business.
- **Networking:** Attending industry events, conferences, and trade shows to meet potential customers.
- **Using Social Media:** Leveraging platforms like LinkedIn, Twitter, and Facebook to connect with potential customers and engage with them.

Step-by-Step Example: Using LinkedIn for Prospecting

- **Define Your Ideal Customer Profile (ICP):** Clearly outline the characteristics of your ideal customers.
- **Search for Prospects:** Use LinkedIn's advanced search to find people who match your ICP.
- **Analyze Profiles:** Look at profiles to gather information on their current role, company, and interests.
- **Send Connection Requests:** Personalize your connection request to increase acceptance rates.
- **Engage with Content:** Like, comment, and share their posts to build rapport.

- **Send a Personalized Message:** Once connected, send a tailored message introducing yourself and explaining how you can provide value.

Example LinkedIn Message:

Hi [Prospect's Name],

I noticed you work at [Company Name] and are involved in [specific role or project]. I believe our [product/service] can help you [specific benefit]. Would you be open to a quick call to discuss further?

Best regards,

[Your Name]

Real-World Example: A Startup's Success Through Strategic Prospecting

A startup named "TechSolutions" began with no customers and limited resources. The founders, Sarah and John, focused on building their customer base through diligent prospecting. They defined their ICP, used LinkedIn to identify key decision-makers in their target industries, and personalized their outreach. They also attended industry events to network and build relationships. Within a year, they had built a solid client base thanks to their strategic approach to prospecting.

Examples of Prospecting

Prospecting can take various forms, including:

- **Researching Companies and Industries:** Identify potential customers by exploring specific industries or markets.

- **Using Social Media:** Leverage platforms like LinkedIn to connect with potential customers and engage with them.
- **Attending Networking Events:** Meet potential customers at industry events, conferences, or trade shows.
- **Using Sales Intelligence Tools:** Gather data on prospects, including contact information and company insights, to tailor your outreach.

Case Study: Prospecting in Action

Let's consider a real-life example of a salesperson, Alex, working for a company that sells marketing automation software.

The Challenge: Alex needs to find new customers in the healthcare industry who have significant marketing teams and use CRM systems.

Approach:

1. **Defining the Ideal Customer Profile (ICP):** Alex's ICP includes companies in the healthcare sector with marketing teams of at least five people using CRM systems and with annual revenues of $10 million or more.
2. **Research and Identification:** Using LinkedIn Sales Navigator, Alex identifies 20 companies that match the ICP criteria and compiles their contact information.
3. **Gathering Insights:** Alex uses sales intelligence tools to learn more about each company's marketing technology stack, recent developments, and key decision-makers.
4. **Personalized Outreach:** Based on this information, Alex crafts personalized emails and prepares for phone calls, addressing specific needs and opportunities for each company.

Example Email:

Hi [Decision-Maker's Name],

I came across [Company Name] and noticed you're using [current marketing technology]. I wanted to reach out and introduce you to our marketing automation software, which can streamline your marketing processes and improve efficiency.

Would you be open to a quick call to discuss further?

Best regards,

Alex

Interactive Elements

Worksheet: Identify Your Ideal Customer Profile (ICP)

- Industry: _______________________
- Company Size: _______________________
- Annual Revenue: _______________________
- Technology Use: _______________________
- Key Decision-Makers: _______________________

Checklist: Effective Prospecting Strategies

- Research target industries and companies
- Utilize social media for connection and engagement
- Attend relevant networking events
- Use sales intelligence tools for detailed company insights
- Personalize outreach messages

Visuals

Include infographics and charts that outline the prospecting process, from identifying potential customers to engaging them. Visual aids can help customers grasp complex information quickly and effectively.

Common Pitfalls and Solutions

1. **Pitfall:** Overgeneralizing the ICP.
   - **Solution:** Regularly update and refine your ICP based on market changes and customer feedback.
2. **Pitfall:** Lack of personalization in outreach.
   - **Solution:** Use data gathered from research and sales intelligence tools to tailor each communication.
3. **Pitfall:** Neglecting follow-up.
   - **Solution:** Implement a systematic follow-up process to stay engaged with prospects. Never let go.

Action Plan: Steps to Effective Prospecting

1. **Define Your ICP:** Clearly outline the characteristics of your ideal customers.
2. **Research and Identify Prospects:** Use tools and resources to find companies and contacts that match your ICP.
3. **Gather Detailed Insights:** Understand each prospect's needs, challenges, and current solutions.
4. **Craft Personalized Outreach:** Develop tailored messages that speak directly to each prospect's situation.
5. **Follow-Up:** Implement a follow-up strategy to maintain engagement and move prospects through the sales funnel.

By following these steps, you can enhance your prospecting efforts and build a strong foundation for sales success. Remember, the goal is not just to identify potential customers but to connect with them meaningfully and move them toward becoming valued clients.

Exercise: Create a List of 10 Prospects

1. Identify ten potential customers based on your ICP.
2. Research each prospect to gather relevant information.
3. Outline a personalized approach for each prospect, including:
   - Introduction
   - Value proposition
   - Call to Action

Let me take you back to the beginning of my sales journey. Picture this - on my first day, management handed me a phone book and said, "Start with the 'A's." What seemed like a mundane task turned out to be a pivotal moment in my career.

At first, flipping through the phone book felt like a simple way to pass the time. But as I made those initial calls, I encountered fears of rejection and uncertainty. Each dial tested my resilience and pushed me out of my comfort zone.

Despite the challenges, this exercise in prospecting became a valuable lesson. It taught me to face rejection head-on, to embrace the unknown, and to persist in the face of adversity. What started as a simple directive turned into a journey of personal growth and professional development.

Step 1: prospecting is not just about making calls; it's about conquering fears, handling rejection, and pushing forward with unwavering determination. Let's embrace this step as a foundation for success in our sales endeavors.

Together, let's step into the world of prospecting with courage and resilience, knowing that each call brings us closer to our goals.

"Concentrate on the activities of prospecting, presenting, and following-up; the sales will take care of themselves."

— Brian Tracy

"Successful prospecting is about making a genuine connection with your prospects."

— Tessa Stowe

Chapter Two: Initial Contact

Steps 1 and 2 go hand in hand. After your prospecting is complete, it's time to initiate contact with your potential customers. For me, this step was the most challenging. The fear of rejection was intense, often causing anxiety and hesitation. However, as I progressed in my sales journey, I realized that overcoming this fear was crucial. With consistency, belief in myself, and confidence in the value of the product I was offering, I learned to manage these feelings and focus on the most important aspect of the process: The Customer.

- Reach out to potential customers via phone, email, or social media
- Introduce yourself and your product/service
- Start building a relationship with the potential Customer. The relationship is the most important part. I would imagine a plastic bubble around the Customer. As an armor, they put up to protect themselves from outside influences. You only have a short time to pop that imaginary bubble. Your words and ability to read the customers' reactions are crucial in this process. Be careful with this step. It is the foundation of the relationship.

Example of step 2: A salesperson sends a personalized email to a decision-maker at a potential customer company, introducing themselves and their product.

Here's an example of step 2, Initial Contact:

Let's say you're a salesperson for a company that sells marketing automation software, and you've identified a potential customer who fits your ideal customer profile (ICP).

You've researched their company and found that they're using a manual process to manage their marketing campaigns, which takes up a lot of time and resources. You've also found that they're struggling to personalize their marketing messages, which is leading to low engagement rates.

You decide to reach out to the potential Customer via email to introduce your product and see if they're interested in learning more. Here's an example email:

"Hi [Decision-Maker's Name],

I came across [Company Name] and noticed you're using a manual process to manage your marketing campaigns. I understand how time-consuming and resource-intensive that can be.

Our marketing automation software can help you streamline your marketing processes and improve efficiency. We've worked with similar companies in the healthcare industry to help them personalize their marketing messages and improve engagement rates.

Would you be open to a quick call to discuss further?

Best,

[Your Name]"

This email is personalized to the potential Customer's specific pain points and interests, and it's brief and to the point. You're not trying to sell them anything yet - you're just trying to open dialog and see if they're interested in learning more.

Here are some other ways you might make initial contact with a potential customer:

- **Phone call:** You could try calling the potential Customer directly to introduce yourself and your product.
- **Social media:** You could try reaching out to the potential Customer on social media platforms like LinkedIn, Instagram, or Twitter.
- **Event:** You could try meeting the potential Customer in person at an industry event or conference.

Remember, the goal of initial contact is to start a conversation and see if the potential Customer is interested in learning more about your product or service. If you are in the sales industry, the Customer is coming directly to you, in your store on your lot, or visiting your website directly. Your presence is your power, as well their presence is their power. In sales, we are only as good as our words, and we must have the ability to communicate effectively. Genuinely introduce yourself and remember you are the individual who cares and wants to serve them.

Key Concepts in Initial Contact

The key to easing anxiety in this stage lies in shifting your focus from yourself to the Customer. It's not about making a sale at this stage; it's about genuinely understanding the Customer's needs and starting to build a relationship. Prioritizing the Customer's interests and well-being diminishes the pressure of rejection. You are there to help, to provide solutions, and to create value. This mindset not only boosts your confidence but also makes the initial contact more authentic and meaningful.

Methods of Initial Contact:

- **Phone:** A direct approach to introduce yourself and your product.
- **Email:** Allows you to provide a clear and thoughtful introduction.
- **Social Media:** Engages customers in a less formal, more interactive way.
- **In-Person Meetings:** Opportunities like industry events or conferences.

Making the Initial Contact

Initial contact involves reaching out to potential customers to introduce yourself and your product or service. This step lays the foundation for a meaningful relationship. Imagine a plastic bubble around the Customer — a protective barrier against outside influences. Your task is to gently but effectively "pop" this bubble, engaging the Customer and demonstrating genuine interest in their needs.

Initial Contact in Action

Let's consider a real-life example of a salesperson, Alex, working for a company that sells marketing automation software. Alex has identified a potential customer, TechHealth, which uses a manual process to manage their marketing campaigns. This process is time-consuming and inefficient. Here's how Alex makes the initial contact:

Initial Contact Email:

Hi [Decision-Maker's Name],

I came across [Company Name] and noticed you're using a manual process to manage your marketing campaigns. I understand how time-consuming and resource-intensive that can be.

Our marketing automation software can help streamline your marketing processes and improve efficiency. We've worked with similar companies in the healthcare industry to personalize their marketing messages and improve engagement rates.

Would you be open to a quick call to discuss further?

Best regards,

Alex

By addressing specific pain points and offering a clear value proposition, Alex opens a dialogue that leads to further engagement and, eventually, a sale.

Example: Successful Initial Contact in Auto Sales

Scenario

Imagine you are a salesperson at an auto dealership. You have identified a potential customer, Mr. Smith, who has shown interest in purchasing a new car through an online inquiry. Here's how you can effectively make initial contact:

Phone Call Script:

Salesperson: Hi, Mr. Smith, this is [Your Name] from [Auto Dealership Name]. I received your inquiry about the [Car Model]. How are you today?

Mr. Smith: I'm good, thank you.

Salesperson: Great to hear! I understand you're interested in the [Car Model]. Love to provide you with more information and answer any questions you may have. Could you tell me a bit about what you're looking for in your next car?

Mr. Smith: Sure, I'm looking for something fuel-efficient and spacious enough for my family.

Salesperson: Excellent; the [Car Model] is known for its fuel efficiency and has plenty of space for a family. It also comes with advanced safety features, which is perfect for family trips. How about we schedule a test drive at your convenience?

Mr. Smith: That sounds good. How about this Saturday?

Salesperson: Saturday works perfectly. I'll set up an appointment for you at 10 am. Thank you for your time, Mr. Smith.

We look forward to seeing you! If, for any reason, my schedule changes, I will give you the courtesy to reach out. Will you do the same for me?

Mr. Smith: Thank you. See you on Saturday at 10 am. I will call you if my schedule changes as well; thank you.

Salesperson: You're welcome. Have a great day!

Interactive Elements

Worksheet: Crafting Your Initial Contact Message

- Identify the Prospect's Pain Points: _________________
- Highlight the Value Proposition: _________________
- Personalize the Message: _________________
- Call to Action: _________________

Checklist: Effective Initial Contact

- Research the prospect thoroughly
- Personalize the message
- Be concise and clear
- Include a call to action
- Prepare for possible responses

Visuals

Include an infographic illustrating the process of crafting an effective initial contact email or message, highlighting key elements such as personalization, value proposition, and call to action. Visuals can help customers quickly understand the structure and key points of a well-crafted outreach message.

Common Pitfalls and Solutions

1. **Pitfall:** Sending generic messages.

   - **Solution:** Personalize each communication based on the prospect's specific needs and company information.
2. **Pitfall:** Being too aggressive or pushy.

- **Solution:** Focus on building a relationship rather than making an immediate sale. Use a consultative approach.
3. **Pitfall:** Lack of follow-up.

- **Solution:** Plan and execute a follow-up strategy to keep the conversation going.

Expert Insights

"Initial contact is not just about reaching out; it's about making a meaningful connection. The most successful salespeople are those who genuinely seek to understand and help their customers."

Action Plan: Steps to Effective Initial Contact

1. **Research Your Prospect:** Understand their business, challenges, and industry.
2. **Personalize Your Approach:** Tailor your message to address their specific needs and pain points.
3. **Be Clear and Concise:** Keep your message brief, focusing on how you can help.
4. **Include a Call to Action:** Invite the prospect to engage further, whether through a call or a meeting.
5. **Follow-up:** Maintain contact and show your commitment to helping them solve their problems.

In sales, effective communication and a genuine desire to help are key. Remember, your presence and engagement are powerful tools. Be sincere, confident, and dedicated to building relationships that go beyond just selling a product.

Practice Initial Contact

I empower you to practice crafting and delivering an initial contact message.

1. Identify the Prospect's Pain Points: _________________
2. Craft an initial contact email or phone script_________________
3. Highlight the Value Proposition: _________________
4. Personalize the Message: _________________
5. Call to Action: _________________
6. Practice delivering the message with a peer or a mentor for feedback._______

Remember, the initial contact is the crucial first step in building a relationship with your prospect. Your sincerity, confidence, and dedication to understanding and helping your customers will set the foundation for a successful sales journey.

Remember:

"You never have to recover from a good start."

— **Drew Houston**

Chapter Three: Qualification

The qualification step is one of the most enjoyable parts of the sales process. This is where you get to listen to your customers, allowing them to express their needs and wants. The more they talk, the better the foundation of your relationship becomes. It's important to remember, "You care." You may only have one shot at demonstrating the value of your product, so listen closely. Customers often reveal how you can meet their needs and even specify the exact product they require. There may be times when the Customer doesn't need what you're selling, making this step crucial for determining fit.

Determine if the potential Customer is a good fit for your product/service:

- Ask questions about their needs, pain points, and goals
- Use the BANT framework (Budget, Authority, Need, Timing) to qualify the lead.

Even though we use the BANT framework, it is more of an internal process/method. We need to determine the Budget. Budget is not a word I like to use in my communication. I prefer the word value over budget. However, it is helpful if you know the Customer's budget. It is more helpful to create value in what they have already spoken to you about in the Qualification step. Could you find the best value for their needs? A customer will always adjust their ideal budget if they see the value in what is being presented.

Authority is self-explanatory. All decision-makers need to be involved to move forward. You could have a great prospect, but that individual is unable to decide to move forward. We need to qualify whether the decision-makers are present or at the very least, available. This sounds simple. However, everyone seems to think they are the decision maker until they are not.

Need and Time act together is the product needed and are we able to deliver in the time it is needed for. Are we as a company able to fulfill our promises to this Customer in a timely fashion and start building on that new relationship?

Example: A salesperson asks a potential customer about their current challenges and goals and determines that they have the budget and authority to make a purchasing decision.

Here's an example of step 3, Qualification:

Let's say you're a salesperson for a company that sells marketing automation software, and you've already made initial contact with a potential customer.

You've scheduled a call with the potential Customer to discuss their marketing challenges and see if your product might be a good fit. During the call, you ask them a series of questions to qualify their needs and determine if they're a good fit for your product.

Here are some examples of qualification questions you might ask:

- What are your biggest marketing challenges right now?
- How are you currently managing your marketing campaigns?

- What are your goals for the next quarter?
- Who else is involved in the decision-making process for marketing technology?
- What is your budget for marketing technology?

Based on the potential Customer's answers, you determine that they:

- Are struggling to personalize their marketing messages
- Are using a manual process to manage their marketing campaigns
- Have a goal to increase lead generation by 20% in the next quarter
- Have a budget of $10,000 for marketing technology
- Have a team of 5 people who will be using the marketing automation software

You also ask some additional questions to determine if your product is a good fit for their needs. For example:

- Are you currently using any other marketing technology platforms?
- How do you currently measure the success of your marketing campaigns?
- Are there any specific features or functionalities that you're looking for in a marketing automation platform?

Based on the potential Customer's answers, you determine that your product is a good fit for their needs and that they are a qualified lead.

Personal Insight

I have always found the qualification step to be the most valuable part of the sales process. This is because of my ability to actively listen and genuinely care about the person in front of me. It's crucial to prioritize the Customer's needs and concerns, as these build trust and rapport. I've often reflected on a quote from a self-help book that deeply resonates with my approach: "People don't care how much you know—until they know how much you care." This sentiment underscores the importance of empathy and genuine interest in the Customer's well-being.

Key Concepts in Qualification

1. **Determine Fit:** Assess if the potential Customer is a good match for your product or service.
2. **Ask Probing Questions:** Understand their needs, pain points, and goals.
3. **Use the BANT Framework:** Evaluate the Budget, Authority, Need, and Timing to qualify the lead.

While the BANT framework is a useful internal tool, the focus should be on understanding and creating value. The word "budget" can be less appealing; consider discussing "value" instead. Customers often adjust their budget if they perceive the value in your offering. Ensure all decision-makers are involved, as this can significantly impact the process. Authority is about identifying decision-makers. Even when a prospect appears to have decision-making power, there may be others involved in the process. Need and Timing often work together; understanding these helps ensure that you can deliver on promises in a timely fashion, laying the groundwork for a lasting relationship.

Qualification in Action

Let's consider a scenario where you're a salesperson for a company that sells marketing automation software. You've made initial contact with a potential customer and scheduled a call to discuss their challenges and how your product might help.

During the call, you ask several questions to qualify their needs and determine if your product is a good fit:

1. What are your biggest marketing challenges right now?
2. How are you currently managing your marketing campaigns?
3. What are your goals for the next quarter?
4. Who else is involved in the decision-making process for marketing technology?
5. What is your budget for marketing technology?

Based on the Customer's responses, you learn that they are struggling with personalization, rely on manual processes, aim to increase lead generation by 20% next quarter, have a $10,000 budget, and have a team of five who will use the software.

Further questions might include:

- Are you currently using any other marketing technology platforms?
- How do you measure the success of your marketing campaigns?
- Are there specific features you're looking for in a marketing automation platform?

Their answers confirm that your product is well-suited to their needs, qualifying them as a lead.

Successful Qualification in Auto Sales

Scenario

Imagine you are a salesperson at an auto dealership. You've had initial contact with a customer, Ms. Johnson, who is interested in buying a new SUV. Here's how you can effectively qualify her needs:

Qualification Conversation:

Salesperson: Hi, Ms. Johnson. I understand you're interested in our latest SUV models. What features are most important to you in a new vehicle?

Ms. Johnson: I need something with a lot of cargo space and good fuel efficiency. Safety features are also a top priority for me.

Salesperson: That makes sense. Could you tell me a bit about how you plan to use the SUV? Are there any specific needs you have in mind?

Ms. Johnson: I have two kids and we do a lot of road trips, so comfort and entertainment options are important as well.

Salesperson: Great, our [SUV Model] offers excellent cargo space, top-notch safety features, and a built-in entertainment system that could be perfect for your family trips. What's your timeline for making a purchase?

Ms. Johnson: Ideally, I'd like to have a new vehicle within the next month.

Salesperson: Wonderful. We have several financing options available to fit different budgets. What range are you considering for your new SUV?

Ms. Johnson: I'm looking to stay within $35,000 to $40,000.

Salesperson: That's very doable. How about we set up a test drive so you can experience the SUV firsthand and see if it meets all your needs? Will 10 am tomorrow work for you?

Ms. Johnson: That sounds perfect. Thank you!

Interactive Elements

Worksheet: Qualification Checklist

- Customer's Main Challenges: ______________________
- Current Solutions in Use: _________________
- Goals and Objectives: _______________
- Decision-Making Authority: ________________
- Budget Considerations: _______________

Self-Assessment: Are You Listening Effectively?

1. Do I allow the Customer to speak freely?
2. Do I ask open-ended questions?
3. Am I focusing on understanding their needs, not just selling?

Visuals An infographic could visually outline the BANT framework, showing how each component (Budget, Authority, Need, Timing) interrelates and contributes to qualifying a lead.

Common Pitfalls and Solutions

1. **Pitfall:** Assuming the prospect understands their own needs.

- **Solution:** Guide the conversation to help uncover deeper needs and potential solutions.
2. **Pitfall:** Overlooking key decision-makers.
   - **Solution:** Always confirm who else is involved in the decision-making process.
3. **Pitfall:** Focusing too much on budget.
   - **Solution:** Emphasize value and ROI, aligning solutions with the Customer's specific pain points and goals.

Expert Insights

"Qualification is not just about checking boxes (although consistency helps); it's about genuinely understanding your prospect's situation and aligning your solution to their unique needs."

Action Plan: Effective Qualification Steps

1. **Prepare Questions in Advance:** Tailor your questions to uncover the prospect's true needs and challenges.
2. **Listen Actively:** Pay close attention to the prospect's responses, noting both explicit needs and underlying concerns.
3. **Confirm Authority and Decision-Making Process:** Ensure all relevant stakeholders are involved or at least informed.
4. **Discuss Value Over Budget:** Focus on how your product can meet their needs and offer value rather than just fitting a budget.
5. **Assess Timing and Need:** Confirm the urgency and relevance of your product to the prospect's current situation.

Qualification is a crucial step in building a trusting and productive relationship with your customers. By focusing on their needs and maintaining open, honest communication, you lay the groundwork for a successful sales process and long-term customer satisfaction.

Exercise: Practice the Qualification Process

Practice the qualification process using active listening and targeted questions.

1. Identify the Prospect's Pain Points: _______________
2. Highlight the Value Proposition: _______________
3. Personalize the Message: _______________
4. Call to Action: _______________

Interactive Worksheet:

- Craft a qualification script that includes open-ended questions to understand the prospect's needs.
- Use active listening techniques during practice sessions with a peer or mentor for feedback.

Encouragement:

Remember, the qualification step is crucial in understanding your Customer's true needs and building a lasting relationship. By focusing on listening and providing value, you can effectively determine if your product or service is the right fit, paving the way for a successful sales journey.

"Qualification is the heart of sales success. It's where you discover if the prospect has a need, and if they do, the salesperson who qualifies best will win."

— Jeffrey Gitomer

Chapter Four: Needs Assessment

I know I said step 3, Qualifying, is the most fun, but they all are, and this step — Needs Assessment — is crucial in combination with step 3. It all comes down to listening and paying attention to how the customer reacts when they speak about their wants and needs. This is where you get the opportunity to pull the information from them that will help you with the building blocks of the sale. How the customer answers your open-ended questions is the bricks that build the foundation. Have fun with this. Get the customer talking—this is your time to let them open up to you.

Key Concepts in Needs Assessment

- **Ask Open-Ended Questions:** Understand the potential customer's needs and pain points.
- **Use Active Listening Skills:** Build rapport and trust.
- **Identify Customer's Goals:** Determine how your product/service can help achieve them.

Personal Insight: In my experience, the Needs Assessment step is immensely rewarding. The ability to actively listen and genuinely care about the customer's needs is paramount. It's important to show that you care about them first. Remember the quote, "People don't care how much you know until they know how much you care." This step is where you can truly demonstrate that.

Example of Needs Assessment

Let's say you're a salesperson for a company that sells marketing automation software, and you've already qualified a lead.

You schedule a call with the lead to conduct a needs assessment and determine how your product can help them achieve their marketing goals.

During the call, you ask open-ended questions to understand the lead's current marketing challenges and goals. For example:

- Can you tell me more about your current marketing strategy?
- How are you currently managing your leads and prospects?
- What are your biggest pain points when it comes to marketing?
- How do you currently measure the success of your marketing campaigns?

The lead shares their current marketing challenges and goals with you, including:

- They're struggling to personalize their marketing messages and are using a manual process to manage their campaigns.
- They're having trouble tracking the success of their campaigns and don't have a clear understanding of their ROI.
- They're looking to increase lead generation by 20% in the next quarter.

You also ask questions about their current marketing technology stack and how they're currently using data and analytics to inform their marketing decisions.

Based on the lead's answers, you identify the following needs:

- They need a marketing automation platform that can help them personalize their marketing messages and streamline their campaign management.
- They need better tracking and analytics capabilities to measure the success of their campaigns and understand their ROI.
- They need a solution that can help them increase lead generation and achieve their marketing goals.

You then use this information to present your product and demonstrate how it can help the lead achieve their marketing goals.

Case Study: Needs Assessment in Action

Consider a scenario where a salesperson from a marketing automation software company is working with a healthcare provider. The provider is currently facing challenges in managing patient outreach and tracking engagement effectively.

Questions Asked:

- Can you describe your current patient engagement strategy?
- What tools are you currently using to manage patient outreach?
- What challenges are you facing in tracking patient engagement and outcomes?

Customer's Needs Identified:

- The healthcare provider needs a more efficient way to manage patient outreach.
- They need better tools for tracking engagement and outcomes.

- They are looking to increase patient engagement by 15% over the next year.

Solution Presented: The salesperson demonstrates how their marketing automation software can streamline patient outreach and provide robust tracking and analytics capabilities, addressing the provider's specific needs and goals.

Interactive Elements

Worksheet: Needs Assessment Checklist

1. Customer's Main Challenges: __________________
2. Current Solutions in Use: __________________
3. Goals and Objectives: __________________
4. Desired Features/Functionalities: __________________
5. Key Decision Makers: __________________

Self-Assessment: Are You Effectively Assessing Needs?

- Do I ask open-ended questions to understand the customer's needs?
- Am I actively listening and showing genuine interest in the customer's responses?
- Do I identify the customer's goals and align my solutions accordingly?

Visuals An infographic could illustrate the process of conducting a needs assessment, highlighting key questions to ask and the flow of information from understanding needs to presenting a solution.

Common Pitfalls and Solutions

1. **Pitfall:** Asking closed-ended questions.

- **Solution:** Focus on open-ended questions that encourage detailed responses.
2. **Pitfall:** Not actively listening.
   - **Solution:** Practice active listening techniques, such as summarizing and reflecting on what the customer says.
3. **Pitfall:** Overlooking key pain points.
   - **Solution:** Probe deeper into the customer's responses to uncover underlying issues and needs.

Expert Insights: "Effective needs assessment is about uncovering the true needs of your customer. It's not just about asking questions; it's about listening, understanding, and responding thoughtfully."

Action Plan: Conducting a Needs Assessment

1. **Prepare Open-Ended Questions:** Tailor your questions to uncover the customer's true needs and challenges.
2. **Practice Active Listening:** Pay close attention to the customer's responses and demonstrate that you value their input.
3. **Identify Goals and Pain Points:** Understand the customer's objectives and the challenges they face in achieving them.
4. **Align Solutions with Needs:** Present your product or service as a solution that directly addresses the customer's needs and goals.
5. **Build Rapport and Trust:** Show genuine interest in the success and build a strong foundation for a lasting relationship.

Exercise: Write a Worksheet to Qualify a Customer's Wants and Needs. Create a worksheet that helps qualify a customer's wants and needs, incorporating active listening skills. Outline specific questions that would help you understand the customer's pain points, goals, and desired features.

Encouragement and Success

Conducting a thorough needs assessment is a crucial step in building a trusting and productive relationship with your customers. By focusing on their needs and maintaining open, honest communication, you lay the groundwork for a successful sales process and long-term customer satisfaction. Remember, the more you understand your customers, the better you can serve them.

"You can have everything in life you want if you will just help enough other people get what they want."

— **Zig Ziglar**

Needs Assessment Checklist Example

Needs Assessment Checklist

Customer Information:

- Customer Name: ________________________
- Company Name: ________________________
- Date: ________________________

Main Challenges:

- What are the main challenges you are currently facing?
    - ○ ________________________
    - ○ ________________________
    - ○ ________________________

Current Solutions in Use:

- What tools or solutions are you currently using to address these challenges?
    - ○ ________________________
    - ○ ________________________

Goals and Objectives:

- What are your primary goals and objectives over the next 6-12 months?

    - ○ ________________________
    - ○ ________________________
    - ○ ________________________

Desired Features/Functionalities:

- What specific features or functionalities are you looking for in a solution?
    - ○ ________________________
    - ○ ________________________

Decision-Making Process:

- Who are the key decision-makers involved in selecting a new solution?
  - _______________________________________
  - _______________________________________

Budget Considerations:

- What is your budget range for this new solution?
  - _______________________________________

Timeline:

- What is your timeline for implementing a new solution?
  - _______________________________________

Customer's Pain Points:

- What are the biggest pain points that your current solution does not address?
  - _______________________________________
  - _______________________________________

Success Metrics:

- How do you measure the success of your current solution?
  - _______________________________________
  - _______________________________________

Product Selection:

- Based on the needs identified, the following products are recommended:
  - Product A:
    - ✓ Features: _______________________________
    - ✓ How it addresses needs:

      ____

  - Product B:
    - ✓ Features: _______________________________

✓ How it addresses needs

____

o Product C:
  ✓ Features:

____

✓ How it addresses needs:

____

Next Steps:

- Schedule a product demo
- Provide a detailed proposal
- Follow-up meeting date: _______________________

Taking Action Toward Product Details and Selection

1. Gather Information:
   - Collect all the details filled out in the checklist.
   - Ensure you have a clear understanding of the Customer's main challenges, goals, and desired features.
2. Match Needs to Products:
   - Review the product options available.
   - Align the Customer's needs and pain points with the features and functionalities of your products.
3. Prepare Recommendations:
   - Select the top 2-3 products that best fit the Customer's needs.
   - Prepare a detailed explanation of how each product addresses its specific challenges and goals.
4. Present Solutions:
   - Schedule a meeting or call to discuss the findings with the Customer.
   - Use the information gathered to present each recommended product, highlighting its benefits and how it meets their needs.
5. Follow-Up:
   - After the Presentation, follow up with the Customer to address any additional questions or concerns.

- Provide any additional information or demos as required.
6. Confirm Decision-Making:
    - Ensure all decision-makers are involved in the discussions.
    - Clarify any remaining points and move towards closing the sale.

By following this checklist and action plan, you can systematically assess the Customer's needs and present the most appropriate products, leading to a more effective and successful sales process.

Chapter Five: Presentation

How exciting is this step? This step is where you can bring your personality, showmanship, salesmanship, and the art of communicating into the sale. It is important to know exactly what you are selling so you can build the most value into that product. The old saying, "A real salesman can sell ice to an Eskimo." is not what I mean. We are not looking to persuade, push, or even manipulate people into buying your product. We are looking to build long-lasting relationships with this company or individual by showing them the value of our product. When you have completed steps 3 (Qualification) and 4 (Needs Assessment) properly, step 5 is pure adrenaline motivated. You already know what the Customer's needs are, so the product you are presenting should be what they need. So, you have to point out all of its VALUE to them.

Showcase your product/service and how it addresses the potential needs. Use demos, trials, or pilots to demonstrate the value of your product/service. Highlight the benefits and features of your product/service.

Personal Insight: In my professional experience, the Presentation step is incredibly exhilarating. It's the culmination of your understanding of the Customer's needs and the moment to shine by showing how your product meets those needs. The energy and excitement you bring to this step can significantly impact the Customer's perception. Remember, it's about building a lasting relationship based on trust and value.

Key Concepts of Product Presentation

1. **Understanding the Customer's Needs:**
   - Review the information gathered during the Qualification and Needs Assessment steps.
   - Tailor your presentation to the specific needs and pain points of the Customer.
2. **Showcasing the Product:**
   - Use demos, trials, or pilots to highlight the key features and benefits of your product.
   - Ensure the Customer understands how your product addresses their specific challenges.
3. **Building Value:**
   - Emphasize the unique value propositions of your product.
   - Use case studies, testimonials, and success stories to reinforce the product's value.
4. **Engaging Showmanship:**
   - Bring energy and enthusiasm to your presentation.
   - Use visuals, storytelling, and interactive elements to keep the Customer engaged.

Example of Step 5: Presentation

Let's say you're a salesperson for a company that sells marketing automation software, and you've already conducted a needs assessment with a lead. You've identified the lead's needs and determined that your product is a good fit to help them achieve their marketing goals. You schedule a call to present your product and demonstrate how it can help the lead.

During the call, you:

1. Introduce your product and its key features.
2. Show a demo of how the product works.

3. Highlight the benefits and value of the product.
4. Share case studies or success stories of similar companies who have used your product.
5. Address any questions or concerns the lead has.

Here's an example script:

"Hello [Customer], thank you for taking the time to speak with me today. I want to introduce you to our marketing automation software, which I believe will help you achieve your marketing goals.

Our software allows you to personalize your marketing messages, streamline your campaign management, and track the success of your campaigns. You can use our software to automate repetitive tasks, such as email marketing and lead nurturing.

I want to show you a demo of how our software works. (Show demo)

As you can see, our software is easy to use and can help you save time and increase efficiency. We've had success with similar companies in the past, such as XYZ Corporation, which saw a 25% increase in lead generation after using our software.

Do you have any questions or concerns about our software?"

The lead asks a few questions, which you address, and then you proceed to the next step in the sales process.

Additional Presentation Methods:

- Use a presentation deck or slides to showcase your product and its features.

- Provide a trial or demo of your product for the lead to try.
- Share testimonials or reviews from satisfied customers.
- Highlight any awards or recognition your product has received.
- Suppose it is a product that the Customer can interact with, show them how it works. Build the excitement and utilize the emotion or euphoria of the new and amazing product. Work on what we call the "SIZZLE."

Here is the rest of the example:

Lead: "That sounds great, but I'm not sure if it's within our budget."

You: "I completely understand. Let me see if I can help with that. Can you tell me a little bit more about your budget and what you're comfortable spending?"

Lead: "We're looking to spend around $1,000 per month."

You: "Okay, great. Well, our software is priced at $1,200 per month, but I can offer you a discount of 10% if you sign up for a year-long contract."

Lead: "That sounds like a good deal. What kind of support do you offer?"

You: "We offer 24/7 support via phone and email, as well as regular software updates and training webinars. We also have a comprehensive knowledge base and community forum where you can connect with other users and get help."

Lead: "That sounds great. I think we're interested in moving forward. What's the next step?"

You: "The next step would be to sign up for a free trial and see how our software works for you. If you're satisfied, we can then discuss pricing and implementation details."

Lead: "Sounds good. Let's do it."

In this example, you:

- Presented the product and its features.
- Addressed the lead's concerns and objections.
- Provided a solution that met the lead's needs and budget.
- Offered support and training to ensure the lead's success.
- Moved the lead to the next step in the sales process (signing up for a free trial).

Case Study: Presentation Success

Situation: A salesperson from a marketing automation software company is working with a healthcare provider. The provider is currently facing challenges in managing patient outreach and tracking engagement effectively.

Action: The salesperson presents a demo of the software, highlighting features like automated patient outreach, personalized messaging, and comprehensive tracking and analytics capabilities.

Result: The healthcare provider sees the potential for increased efficiency and improved patient engagement, leading to a decision to move forward with a trial of the software.

Interactive Elements

Worksheet: Presentation Preparation Checklist

- Key Features of Your Product: _______________________
- Customer's Needs Addressed: _______________________
- Demo Script Outline: _______________________
- Case Studies or Success Stories to Share: _______________________
- Anticipated Questions and Responses: _______________________

Self-Assessment: Are You Ready to Present?

- Have I tailored my presentation to the specific needs and pain points of the Customer?
- Do I know my product inside and out?
- Am I prepared to address potential objections and concerns?

Common Pitfalls and Solutions

- **Pitfall:** Overloading the Customer with information.
  - **Solution:** Focus on the key features and benefits that address the Customer's specific needs.
- **Pitfall:** Not addressing the Customer's concerns.
  - **Solution:** Be prepared to listen to and address any questions or objections the Customer may have.
- **Pitfall:** Failing to demonstrate the product.
  - **Solution:** Use demos, trials, or pilots to show the product in action and highlight its value.

Expert Insights

"Effective presentations are not just about showcasing your product; they're about connecting with your audience and addressing their unique needs and concerns."

Action Plan: Preparing for Your Presentation

1. **Understand the Customer's Needs:** Review the information gathered during the Qualification and Needs Assessment steps.
2. **Prepare Your Demo:** Highlight the key features and benefits of your product that address the Customer's specific needs.
3. **Practice Your Presentation:** Rehearse your demo and script to ensure a smooth delivery.
4. **Anticipate Objections:** Be prepared to address common concerns and questions the Customer may have.
5. **Follow-Up:** After the presentation, follow up with the Customer to address any additional questions and move to the next step in the sales process.

Challenge to the Reader

Write a Script: Create a script that helps present the product to customers, mirroring their wants and needs. Incorporate showmanship and detailed explanations to complete a proper presentation or walk around of the product you are selling.

Example Script of Successful Presentation

"Hello [Customer], thank you for taking the time to meet with me today. I'm excited to show you our latest product, which I believe aligns perfectly with the needs and goals you shared with us.

As we discussed, your primary challenges are [list challenges]. Our product addresses these challenges by [explain how]—for instance, [demonstrate a key feature], which will help you [explain benefit].

Let's dive into a demo to see it in action. (Conduct demo)

As you can see, the intuitive interface and powerful features can significantly improve your workflow and efficiency. We've seen similar success with companies like [mention case study], who experienced [specific result].

Do you have any questions or concerns so far? (Address questions)

To move forward, I recommend starting with our trial period to see firsthand how it can benefit your operations. We offer comprehensive support to ensure a smooth transition and maximize your success with our product.

Thank you for your time today. I'm confident this solution will meet your needs and look forward to working with you."

Presenting your product is a thrilling step in the sales process. It's your opportunity to showcase the value you've identified and connect with your customers on a deeper level. Remember, confidence, enthusiasm, and a thorough understanding of your product will shine through and leave a lasting impression. Success in this step lays the foundation for a strong relationship and future opportunities.

"No one cares how much you know until they know how much you care."

— Theodore Roosevelt

Chapter Six: Handling Objections

Handling objections is a critical part of the sales process that improves with consistency and practice. I once worked with a sales professional named James, who was a happy, quiet individual that everyone enjoyed being around. However, he struggled to sell the product and was on the brink of losing his job. With the help of a veteran mentor, Carlos, James adopted a consistent approach to selling—doing the same thing every time, asking the same questions, and consistently demonstrating the product. His sales quickly increased. Just like Michael Jordan didn't become great at basketball overnight, mastering the skill of handling objections requires consistent effort and the drive to improve.

Key Concepts of Handling Objections

1. **Anticipate Objections:** By anticipating objections, you can prepare responses that address customer concerns before they even voice them. This proactive approach demonstrates your understanding of their needs and positions you as a knowledgeable and trusted advisor.
2. **Use the FEEL-FELT-FOUND Framework:** This is a classic approach to handling objections:
   a. **FEEL:** Acknowledge the Customer's feelings.
   b. **FELT:** Empathize by sharing that others have felt the same way.

    c. **FOUND:** Present what others have found after using the product.

3. **Offer Solutions and Alternatives:** Provide solutions or alternatives that directly address the Customer's concerns. This might include offering a different package, highlighting a unique feature, or providing additional support.

Example of Handling Objections

Let's say you're a salesperson for a company that sells project management software, and you're in a meeting with a potential customer who is interested in your product but has some concerns.

Potential Customer: "I like the features of your software, but I'm worried it will be too complicated for my team to learn. We don't have a lot of technical expertise."

You: "I completely understand your concern. However, our software is designed to be user-friendly and intuitive. We also offer comprehensive training and support to ensure a smooth transition. Most of our customers are up and running within a week. And, we have a customer success team that is always available to help. Would you like me to show you some examples of how our software can be customized to fit your team's needs?"

In this example, you:

- Acknowledged the potential Customer's concern (FEEL)
- Empathized with their perspective (FELT)
- Provided a solution to address their concern (FOUND)

By using the FEEL-FELT-FOUND framework, you were able to handle the objection and provide a solution that addresses the potential Customer's concern.

Common Objections and How to Handle Them

1. **"Your product is too expensive."**
   - **Response:** "I understand budget is a concern (FEEL). Many of our clients initially felt the same way (FELT), but they found that the efficiency and time savings our product provides more than justified the cost (FOUND). Let me show you how it can save you money in the long run."
2. **"We already have a solution in place."**
   - **Response:** "That makes sense (FEEL). Other clients felt the same (FELT), but they found that our product offered unique features that enhanced their current solution (FOUND). Can I show you how it could integrate seamlessly with what you're already using?"
3. **"I need to think about it."**
   - **Response:** "I completely understand wanting to make the right decision (FEEL). Many of our clients felt the same (FELT), but they found that acting quickly allowed them to start seeing benefits sooner (FOUND). What specific concerns can I address to help with your decision?"
4. **"We don't have the time to implement something new."**
   - **Response:** "I hear you (FEEL). Several of our clients felt overwhelmed at first (FELT), but they found that our product was quick to implement and actually saved them time in the long run (FOUND). I can walk you through the process."
5. **"I'm not the decision-maker."**
   - **Response:** "I appreciate you letting me know (FEEL). Other clients in your position felt the same (FELT), but

they found that our product made such a compelling case that it was easy to get buy-in from decision-makers (FOUND). Would it help if we set up a meeting with all stakeholders?"

Case Studies: The Value of Handling Objections

Case Study 1: Overcoming Price Objections

- **Situation:** A customer is concerned about the cost of marketing automation software.
- **Action:** The salesperson listens to the Customer's concern about budget and asks, "If price wasn't an issue, would you agree that our software would provide the ROI your company is looking for?" When the Customer agrees, the salesperson revisits the product's benefits and ROI potential and then discusses flexible payment options.
- **Result:** The Customer understands the long-term value and signs up for a yearly contract.

Case Study 2: Addressing Complexity Concerns

- **Situation:** A healthcare provider is hesitant to adopt new patient management software due to perceived complexity.
- **Action:** The salesperson empathizes with the concern, uses the FEEL-FELT-FOUND framework, and demonstrates the software's ease of use, coupled with robust customer support.
- **Result:** The healthcare provider is reassured and decides to proceed with the software implementation.

Interactive Exercise: Practice Handling Objections

Exercise: Write responses to the five most common objections you encounter. Use the FEEL-FELT-FOUND framework for each one. Role-play these scenarios with a colleague or mentor, focusing on maintaining a calm, empathetic tone and providing solutions that address the Customer's needs.

Example: Handling Price Objections

Let's say you're a salesperson for a company that sells marketing automation software, and you've already demonstrated your product to the Customer.

Potential Customer: "I love the product, but I'm not sure if it's within our budget. Can you do anything to help with the price?"

You: "I completely understand. Let me ask you, 'If price wasn't the issue, would you agree that our product would provide your company with the ROI results you are looking for?'"

(Pause)

If the Customer says "NO," then you need to go back to step 5 (Presenting the product) and continue building value. If you start talking price before the client sees the value, they will NEVER pay the price you set.

If the customer answers "YES," revisit the benefits of the product to their company and the ROI they will retain. Once you do, determine what the true budget concern is: the monthly fee, the initial investment, or the entire cost of the product. From there, based on your sales skills, redirect the attention to the money they are losing by not having the product at hand currently. When they implement the change of product to their company, the ROI will generate profit growth to pay for the product and cultivate exponential growth in the future.

Most would jump right into saying, "Okay, I can offer you a discount of 10% if you sign up for a year-long contract. Would that help?" No, that will lead to a devaluation of the product. Why wouldn't you have just started with the discounted price (this is what may be going through the consumer's mind)?

Your strategic plan would be to include an additional upgraded package at the same price. Providing the Customer with more options, accessibility, support, and training of the product will shift the mindset of the client's perceived value of the product. The old saying, "More for Less."

The lead thinks for a moment and then says: "Okay, that sounds good. I think we can make it work."

If the client continues to press for a discount, see if the product can be discounted or have a free trial period, pending the product you are selling. This potential discount should already have been considered in your mind before the proposal. Smooth communication and having answers available without research give a transparent projection.

In this example, you:

- Acknowledged the Customer's concern about the price
- Provided additional value (support and training) to increase the product value

- Offered a solution (discount) to help address the concern if needed
- Closed the sale by addressing the Customer's final concerns

Encouragement and Success

Handling objections is a crucial step in the sales process. It's not about pushing back against the Customer's concerns but rather understanding their perspective and guiding them toward a solution that fits their needs. Consistent practice and a positive attitude will transform objections into opportunities to reinforce the value of your product and build stronger relationships with your customers.

Challenge: Script Your Responses

Your challenge is to write a script for handling the five most common objections you face in your sales process. Focus on using the FEEL-FELT-FOUND framework and providing clear, concise solutions that address the Customer's concerns.

Motivational Quote

"Objections are not stop signs; they are guidelines."

— Bo Bennett

Chapter Seven: Demonstration

The Demonstration step is similar to the Presentation but adds another layer of value by allowing the Customer to experience your product firsthand. In various sales fields, this might involve an extended test drive, a free trial, or a complete walk-around of the unit. This step is your opportunity to engage the Customer deeply, showcasing the features, benefits, and overall value of your product.

Key Concepts of Demonstration

1. **Provide a Demo or Trial**: Allow the potential Customer to experience your product or service. This firsthand interaction builds trust and credibility, giving them a tangible sense of how your product will meet their needs.
2. **Showcase Features and Benefits**: During the demo, focus on how the product solves the Customer's specific challenges. Highlight the features that are most relevant to their needs.
3. **Engage the Customer**: Make the demo interactive. Encourage the Customer to ask questions and interact with the product. This not only keeps them engaged but also helps address any concerns they might have.
4. **Tailor the Demo**: Customize the demonstration to align with the Customer's specific pain points and objectives. This tailored approach enhances the relevance and impact of your Presentation.
5. **Use Real-Life Examples**: Share case studies or success stories that illustrate how your product has helped other customers achieve their goals.

Example: Demonstration

Let's say you're a salesperson for a company that sells marketing automation software, and you've already presented your product to a customer. The Customer is interested in learning more about how your product works and has asked for a demonstration. You schedule a call and share your screen to show the Customer how to use your product.

During the demo, you:

- Walk through how to log in and navigate the dashboard, indicating the ease and quickness from one task to the next.
- Demonstrate how to create and automate marketing campaigns.
- Show how to track and analyze results.
- Highlight the features and benefits of your product.

This is selling the "Sizzle." Wow, the Customer and present with enthusiasm and excitement while being completely genuine in the process.

Example Script: You: "Okay, let me show you how to log in and get started." (Share screen and show login process)

You: "Once you're logged in, you can navigate to the dashboard and see an overview of your campaigns." (Show dashboard)

You: "Let me show you how to create a new campaign." (Show campaign creation process)

You: "You can choose from a variety of templates and customize the content to fit your needs." (Show template options)

You: "Once you've created your campaign, you can automate it to run on its own." (Show automation options)

You: "You can also track and analyze the results of your campaigns to see what's working and what's not." (Show reporting options)

You: "We also have a variety of integrations with other marketing tools to help you streamline your workflow." (Show integrations)

You: "Do you have any questions so far?"

The Customer hopefully will ask a few questions, which you address, and then you proceed to the next step in the sales process.

Five Most Common Success Practices in Demonstrating Your Product

1. **Engage Early and Often**: Start by engaging the Customer right from the beginning of the demo. Ask questions to understand their immediate needs and expectations.
2. **Focus on the Customer's Pain Points**: Tailor the demo to address the specific challenges the Customer is facing directly. Highlight how your product can solve these issues.
3. **Keep It Simple and Concise**: Avoid overwhelming the Customer with too much information. Please focus on the most relevant features and benefits that will make a difference for them.
4. **Use Real-Life Examples and Case Studies**: Demonstrate how your product has successfully helped others. Real-world applications make the demo more relatable and convincing.
5. **Be Ready to Adapt**: Be flexible during the demo. If the Customer shows interest in a particular feature, spend more

time on it, or if they seem disengaged, pivot to something that might capture their attention better.

Case Study: Effective Product Demonstration

- **Situation**: A sales representative for a marketing automation software company schedules a demo with a potential customer who is interested but unsure about the product's usability.
- **Action**: The sales representative walks the Customer through the software's login, navigation, campaign creation, automation, and reporting features, emphasizing user-friendliness and integration capabilities.
- **Result**: The Customer gains confidence in the software's ease of use and comprehensive features, leading to a successful sale.

Personal Reflection

Properly demonstrating a product is crucial because it ensures that you focus on what the Customer truly needs. As a salesperson, it's easy to get lost in your Presentation, spending too much time on aspects of the product that you find valuable but that the Customer may not. This misalignment can lead to losing the Customer's attention and possibly the sale entirely.

I've learned this firsthand. Early in my career, I once spent an entire demo highlighting a feature I thought was groundbreaking. The potential Customer seemed polite but disengaged. It wasn't until later that I realized I had ignored the features that would have directly addressed their pain points. That experience taught me the importance of aligning my demonstration with the Customer's needs and interests.

Remember, the key is to listen actively to your Customer's needs and tailor your demonstration to showcase how your product addresses those needs. This approach not only keeps the Customer engaged but also builds trust and increases the likelihood of a successful sale.

Exercise: Demonstration Practice

Worksheet: Product Demonstration Preparation

1. List the key features you want to demonstrate:
   ____

2. Create a clear and concise script for the demo:
   ____

3. Prepare case studies or comparisons to illustrate benefits:
   ____

4. Plan for potential questions and concerns:
   ____

Self-Assessment: Ready for a Demo?

- Have I prepared a clear and concise demo script?
- Am I familiar with all the key features of the product?
- Do I have examples or case studies ready to share?
- Am I prepared to answer potential customer questions?

Encouragement

Demonstrating your product is not just about showing off features; it's about connecting with your Customer and showing them how your product can solve their problems and improve their business. A well-executed demo builds trust, showcases value, and can turn a prospect into a loyal customer. Master this skill, and you'll find that the demonstration step is one of the most powerful tools in your sales arsenal.

Motivational Quote

"The goal of this presentation is to impress, rather than to inform."

— William Rushton

Proposal Presentation Checklist: Highlighting Value

1. **Understanding the Customer's Needs**
   - Review the Customer's key pain points and needs.
   - Align your proposal with these specific requirements.
2. **Customize the Proposal**
   - Tailor your proposal to reflect the Customer's unique situation.
   - Highlight features and benefits most relevant to the Customer.
3. **Clearly Outline the Value Proposition**
   - Begin with a clear statement of the value your product brings.
   - Emphasize how your product solves the Customer's problems or enhances their operations.
4. **Present Pricing and ROI**
   - Provide a transparent breakdown of pricing.
   - Include an ROI analysis or value-for-money comparison.
5. **Use Supporting Data and Metrics**
   - Include case studies, testimonials, or success stories that illustrate the product's effectiveness.
   - Present data that supports your claims, such as performance metrics or user satisfaction rates.
6. **Anticipate and Address Objections**
   - Preemptively answer common objections related to cost, implementation, or compatibility.
   - Offer solutions or alternatives within the proposal.
7. **Provide a Clear Implementation Plan**
   - Outline how the product will be integrated or delivered.
   - Include a timeline, support options, and key milestones.
8. **Keep the Proposal Clear and Concise**
   - Avoid overwhelming the Customer with unnecessary information.
   - Focus on the most critical points that demonstrate value.

9. **Engage the Customer During the Presentation**
   - Invite questions and encourage dialogue to ensure understanding.
   - Be prepared to adapt your Presentation based on the Customer's feedback.

10. **Close with a Call to Action**
   - Clearly state the next steps, whether it's signing a contract, scheduling a follow-up, or beginning implementation.
   - Reinforce the value one last time before concluding.

Chapter Eight: Proposal

The proposal step is a thoughtful presentation that should focus on the value of the product and the structure of how the product will be paid for.

- **Present a customized solution and pricing** to the potential Customer, whether monthly, cash difference, or a one-payment plan.
- **Highlight the benefits and value** of your product/service.
- **Use data and metrics** to support your proposal.

Example: Proposal

Let's say you're a salesperson for a company that sells marketing automation software, and you've already handled the Customer's objections. You're now ready to present a proposal to the lead, outlining the terms of the sale.

Example Script:

You: "Okay, [Customer name], I think we've covered all the bases. Here's a proposal outlining the terms of the sale:

- **Product**: Marketing Automation Software
- **Price**: $1,000 per month (with a 10% discount for a year-long contract)
- **Support and Training**: Included
- **Implementation**: We'll provide a dedicated implementation specialist to ensure a smooth onboarding process
- **Timeline**: We can have you up and running within two weeks

"Is this something you're comfortable with? Do you have any questions or concerns?"

The lead reviews the proposal and asks a few questions, which you address. Then, they say:

Customer: "Yes, this looks good. Let's do it!"

You've now closed the sale and can move on to the next step, which is to deliver the product and ensure customer satisfaction.

Additional Tips for Presenting a Proposal

- Be clear and concise in your proposal.
- Include all necessary details, such as price, support, and implementation.
- Use a professional format and layout.
- Be prepared to answer questions or concerns the Customer may have.
- Reinforce the value and benefits of your product.

Personal Reflection

Proposals are pivotal moments in the sales process where you summarize the value and benefits of your product while addressing the financial aspects. One of the most critical lessons I've learned is to customize each proposal to reflect the unique needs and priorities of the Customer. Early in my career, I made the mistake of using a one-size-fits-all approach, and I often missed key details that mattered most to my clients. It wasn't until I started tailoring my proposals that I saw a significant increase in closing rates. Taking the time to understand and address the Customer's specific needs not only shows that you value their business but also builds trust and credibility.

Case Study: Personalized Proposals

- **Situation**: A salesperson for a software company is ready to present a proposal to a potential customer after addressing their objections.
- **Action**: The salesperson creates a personalized proposal outlining the specific benefits and ROI of the product, including detailed pricing and implementation plans.
- **Result**: The Customer feels confident in the proposal's value and agrees to the terms, leading to a successful sale.

Interactive Elements

Worksheet: Proposal Preparation

1. **Identify key customer needs and priorities**:
   ____

2. **List the main benefits of your product** for this specific Customer: _________________

3. **Outline the pricing structure and payment options**:
   ____

4. **Prepare data and metrics** to support your proposal:
   ____

5. **Draft a clear and concise proposal**: _________________

Self-Assessment: Ready to Present a Proposal?

- Have I customized the proposal to reflect the Customer's needs?

- Is the pricing structure clear and detailed?
- Have I included all the necessary details, such as support and implementation plans?
- Am I prepared to answer potential customer questions?

Visuals

An infographic could illustrate the components of a successful proposal, such as product details, pricing, support, and implementation.

Common Pitfalls and Solutions

1. **Pitfall**: Failing to customize the proposal.
   - **Solution**: Take the time to understand the Customer's unique needs and priorities and tailor the proposal accordingly.
2. **Pitfall**: Overcomplicating the proposal with too much information.
   - **Solution**: Keep the proposal clear and concise, focusing on the most important details.
3. **Pitfall**: Not addressing potential objections.
   - **Solution**: Anticipate and address any concerns the Customer may have within the proposal.

Expert Insights

"A well-crafted proposal is not just about listing features and prices; it's about painting a picture of success for your customer."

Action Plan: Mastering Proposals

1. **Research and Understand Customer Needs**: Gather as much information as possible about the Customer's specific needs and priorities.

2. **Customize Your Proposal**: Tailor your proposal to address the unique needs and challenges of the Customer.
3. **Be Clear and Concise**: Present the proposal in a clear, professional format, highlighting the key details.
4. **Use Supporting Data and Metrics**: Include data and metrics to reinforce the value and benefits of your product.
5. **Be Prepared to Address Questions and Concerns**: Anticipate potential questions and objections and be ready with answers.

By consistently preparing and customizing your proposals, you can enhance your credibility, build stronger relationships with your customers, and increase your chances of closing the sale.

Chapter Nine: Negotiation

Negotiation is a critical step in the sales process that could warrant an entire book of its own. Effective negotiation involves clear and consistent communication, treating your Customer with respect, and maintaining focus on their needs and how your product can benefit them. It's essential to take your wants for sale out of the equation and concentrate on building a relationship based on mutual benefit.

Key items to focus on during negotiation:

- **Collaborate** with the potential Customer to reach a mutually beneficial agreement.
- **Use active listening** skills to understand their needs and concerns.
- **Be flexible** and willing to compromise.

Example: Negotiation

Let's say you're a salesperson for a company that sells marketing automation software, and you've already presented a proposal to the Customer. They are interested in purchasing your product but want to negotiate the price.

Customer: "I love the product, but I was thinking more along the lines of $800 per month. Can you do anything to meet me in the middle?"

You: "I understand where cost is always a concern." (Notice we open by acknowledging the concern.) Your goal here is not to immediately discount the price. Redirect the focus back onto the product and its value. The best news in this example is the Customer made an offer. Although their offer is $200 less than your price, you would continue with something along these lines (after a pause):

"Mr. Customer, I am glad you noticed the value of the product. The proposal is with an already market-adjusted price based on your needs to increase the Revenue of your business. I would be honored to offer you a 3-month reduced trial rate of $900, saving you $100 per month for the first three months. After three months, the product will be billed at the initial monthly rate. Additionally, I can include an extra support and training program to help you get the most out of the product for a quicker profit increase."

Customer: "That sounds good, but I'm still a bit stretched thin on budget. Can you do any better?"

This is the Customer's way of reaching for additional discounts or savings. The Customer sees the value in your product because they are still engaged. This is the time to ask for the sale.

You: "Mr. Customer, I see you are captivated by the growth this program can provide your company and recognize the value it will bring. If I reduce the price to $900 for a two-year contract, would that work for you?" (Pause)

The Customer agrees, and you've successfully negotiated the price. Immediately shake your Customer's hand and thank them for the business and new relationship.

Additional Tips for Negotiations

- **Listen carefully** to the Customer's concerns and respond thoughtfully.
- **Be flexible** and willing to compromise.
- **Use the Feel-Felt-Found framework** to acknowledge the Customer's concerns and provide a solution.
- **Use the That's-Not-All technique** or even the Yes-And technique to provide additional value and sweeten the deal.
- **Be transparent and clear** about your pricing and any discounts you're offering.

Personal Reflection

Negotiation is more than just discussing numbers; it's about understanding and addressing the Customer's needs while maintaining the value of your product. Early in my career, I focused too much on my desire to close the sale and often failed to listen to what the Customer truly needed. This approach cost me several deals. Once I shifted my focus to understanding the Customer's perspective and collaborating to find a solution that worked for both parties, my success rate in negotiations improved dramatically.

I also learned that when a customer is primarily focused on price, it often means they haven't fully grasped the value of the product. In such cases, I found it crucial to confirm they understand the value and then redirect the conversation toward the results the product can deliver and how it can solve their problems. If you can demonstrate how your product solves a problem, you can create a customer for life.

Case Study: Effective Negotiation

- **Situation**: A salesperson for a software company is ready to negotiate the price with a potential customer after presenting a proposal.
- **Action**: The salesperson actively listens to the Customer's budget concerns and offers a reduced trial rate and additional support, eventually agreeing on a two-year contract with a slightly reduced price.
- **Result**: The Customer feels valued and agrees to the terms, leading to a successful sale and a strong foundation for a long-term relationship.

Interactive Elements

Worksheet: Negotiation Preparation

1. **Identify key customer concerns and needs**: __________________
2. **List the main benefits of your product** that address these concerns: __________________
3. **Prepare potential compromise options**: __________________
4. **Draft responses using the Feel-Felt-Found framework**: __________________
5. **Practice your negotiation script**: __________________

Self-Assessment: Ready to Negotiate?

- Have I identified the Customer's key concerns?
- Do I have potential compromise options prepared?
- Am I ready to use active listening and respond thoughtfully?
- Have I practiced my negotiation script?

Visuals

An infographic could illustrate the key steps in a successful negotiation, such as active listening, collaborating on solutions, and finalizing the agreement.

Common Pitfalls and Solutions

1. **Pitfall**: Failing to listen to the Customer.
   - **Solution**: Use active listening skills and acknowledge their concerns.
2. **Pitfall**: Being inflexible in negotiations.
   - **Solution**: Prepare multiple options and be willing to compromise.
3. **Pitfall**: Rushing to close the sale.
   - **Solution**: Focus on building a relationship and finding a mutually beneficial solution.

Expert Insights

"Successful negotiation isn't about winning at all costs; it's about finding a solution that works for both parties and fosters a long-term relationship."

Action Plan: Mastering Negotiation

1. **Research and Understand Customer Needs**: Gather information about the Customer's specific needs and priorities.
2. **Prepare Multiple Options**: Have different compromise options ready to address various concerns.
3. **Use Active Listening**: Listen carefully to the Customer's concerns and respond thoughtfully.

4. **Be Clear and Transparent**: Ensure your pricing and discounts are clear and understandable.

5. **Focus on Building Relationships**: Remember, the goal is to create a long-term relationship, not just make a quick sale.

Here are ten tips on how to successfully write a practice script for negotiations:

1. **Know Your Objective:**
   - Clearly define what you want to achieve in the negotiation. Whether it's closing a deal at a specific price or securing a long-term contract, your script should align with your end goal.

2. **Understand the Customer's Needs:**
   - Start by identifying the key needs and concerns of the Customer. Your script should address these points directly, showing empathy and understanding of their position.

3. **Incorporate Active Listening:**
   - Include pauses in your script where you anticipate the Customer will respond. Plan how you'll acknowledge their statements, using phrases like "I hear you," "That's a valid point," or "Let's explore that further."

4. **Highlight Your Value Proposition:**
   - Clearly articulate the unique value your product or service offers. Focus on how it solves the Customer's problems or meets their needs better than alternatives.

5. **Plan for Objections:**
   - Anticipate common objections and prepare responses. Use the Feel-Felt-Found framework (e.g., "I understand how you feel; others have felt the same way, but they found that...") to navigate these objections smoothly.

6. **Be Flexible:**
   - Your script should include multiple options or paths depending on the Customer's reactions. Be ready to offer compromises or alternative solutions that still align with your objectives.

7. **Use Clear and Concise Language:**
   - Avoid jargon or overly complex language. Your script should be easy to follow, with clear points that the Customer can easily understand.

8. **Practice Empathy:**
   - Include statements that show you understand the Customer's perspective. This helps build rapport and makes the Customer more likely to work with you towards a solution.

9. **Close with Confidence:**
   - Plan how you'll ask for the sale or agreement at the end of the negotiation. This should be done confidently, summarizing the benefits and asking a direct, clear question (e.g., "Does that sound like a fair agreement?").

10. **Review and Revise:**
   - After writing your script, review it for any potential weaknesses or unclear areas. Consider role-playing with a colleague to refine your approach and ensure you're prepared for various scenarios.

Chapter Ten: Closing

Closing the sale is often the most exhilarating part of the sales process. It's the moment when all your hard work pays off, and you bring the customer relationship to fruition. But closing isn't just about sealing the deal; it's about solidifying trust and laying the groundwork for a long-term partnership.

Key Concepts of Closing a Sale

1. **Recapping Value:** Reiterate the key benefits and value of the product that the Customer has agreed upon.
2. **Asking for the Sale:** Be direct and confident when asking the Customer to commit.
3. **Handling Last-Minute Objections:** Be prepared to address any final concerns that may arise before closing.
4. **Finalizing Details:** Confirm all the terms, conditions, and next steps to ensure a smooth transition.
5. **Building Relationships:** Focus on establishing a foundation for a long-term relationship by expressing appreciation and setting the stage for future interactions.

Five Common Success Practices for Closing Techniques

1. **The Summary Close:** Recap all the agreed-upon benefits to reinforce the value before asking for the sale.
2. **The Assumptive Close:** Act as if the Customer has already decided to buy and proceed with the closing steps.

3. **The Urgency Close:** Create a sense of urgency by highlighting limited availability or time-sensitive offers.
4. **The Trial Close:** Ask a question that assumes the Customer is ready to buy, such as, "Would you prefer the standard or premium package?"
5. **The Alternative Close:** Offer the Customer a choice between two or more options, leading them to a decision.

Example: Successfully Closing a Sale

Imagine you're a salesperson for a company selling marketing automation software. You've already negotiated the price and addressed the Customer's needs. Now, it's time to close the sale.

You: "Mr. Customer, I'm thrilled we've aligned on the $900 per month for the two-year contract, including the extra support and training. To confirm, you'll be getting access to all the advanced features that will streamline your marketing efforts and boost your ROI. Are you ready to move forward and sign the agreement?"

Customer: "Yes, that sounds good."

You: "Fantastic! Let's finalize the paperwork. I'll send over the contract for your signature, and once that's done, we can get you on board and start driving results."

By confidently summarizing the value and asking for commitment, you've successfully closed the sale, ensuring the Customer is excited about the future relationship.

Case Study: Effective Closing

- **Situation:** A salesperson is finalizing a deal with a customer interested in a software solution. The Customer has expressed interest but hesitates to commit.
- **Action:** The salesperson uses the Assumptive Close technique, proceeding as if the Customer is ready to buy. They confidently reap the benefits and ask, "Shall I send over the contract for your signature now?"
- **Result:** The Customer, feeling reassured and supported, agrees to sign the contract. The salesperson successfully closes the deal, setting up a long-term partnership.

Interactive Elements

Worksheet: Closing Preparation

- **Confirm the agreed terms:** Write down all the terms you've discussed and agreed upon with the Customer.
- **Prepare a clear and concise closing script:** Develop a script that summarizes the key benefits and directly asks for the sale.
- **Ensure all necessary details are covered:** Create a checklist of all-important details that need to be confirmed before finalizing the sale.
- **Outline the next steps for onboarding:** Plan out the steps for onboarding the Customer after the sale is closed.
- **Practice your closing script:** Role-play your script with a colleague or mentor to refine your delivery.

Self-Assessment: Ready to Close?

- Have I confirmed all agreed terms?
- Do I have a clear and concise closing script?
- Are all necessary details covered?

- Have I outlined the next steps for onboarding?
- Am I ready to ask for the sale confidently?

Visuals

An infographic could illustrate the key steps in successfully closing a sale:

1. **Recap Value:** Reinforce the benefits discussed.
2. **Ask for the Sale:** Be clear and direct in your request.
3. **Handle Objections:** Address any last-minute concerns.
4. **Finalize Details:** Ensure everything is agreed upon.
5. **Build Relationships:** Set the stage for an ongoing partnership.

Expert Insights

"Closing a sale is not the end of the process, but the beginning of a relationship. Ensuring a smooth transition and clear communication sets the foundation for long-term success."

Expert's Insight: Effective closers understand that the end of one sale is the start of another opportunity. Each closed sale is a step in building a stronger customer relationship.

Reflective Paragraph

Closing a sale is more than just completing a transaction; it's about establishing a relationship built on trust and mutual respect. The way you close can set the tone for the entire relationship. By focusing on the Customer's needs, confidently asking for the sale, and ensuring a smooth transition, you lay the groundwork for a partnership that can last for years. Remember, closing the deal is just the beginning of a journey where you continue to support and add value to your Customer's business.

Motivational Quote

"Closing the sale is just the beginning of a relationship, not the end."

— Zig Ziglar

Here are 20 commonly practiced closing techniques, along with their purposes in building value and trust:

1. **Assumptive Close**: This technique involves assuming the prospect is ready to buy and moving forward with the next steps. It builds confidence and demonstrates belief in the product's value, which can instill trust.

2. **Alternative Choice Close**: Offering two or more choices for the prospect to choose from (e.g., "Would you prefer the standard or premium package?"). This technique builds value by highlighting options and gives the prospect a sense of control, which fosters trust.

3. **Trial Close**: Asking questions to gauge the prospect's readiness to buy (e.g., "How do you feel about moving forward with this solution?"). It helps in understanding the prospect's position and builds trust by showing respect for their decision-making process.

4. **Urgency Close**: Creating a sense of urgency (e.g., "This offer is only available for the next 24 hours"). It emphasizes the value of acting quickly and helps build trust by demonstrating limited availability and genuine opportunity.

5. **Summary Close**: Summarize the key benefits and features of the product or service before asking for the sale. This reinforces the value and helps build trust by ensuring the prospect has all the necessary information to make a decision.

6. **Direct Close**: Simply asking for the sale directly (e.g., "Are you ready to move forward with this purchase?"). It shows confidence in the product and builds trust through straightforward communication.

7. **Soft Close**: Using a gentle approach to ask for the sale (e.g., "Would you like to get started with this plan today?"). It builds value by focusing on the prospect's comfort level and shows respect for their decision-making process.

8. **Columbo Close**: Asking a question after presenting the solution (e.g., "Just one more thing—how do you feel about this solution?"). It builds trust by addressing any last concerns and demonstrating thoroughness.

9. **Ben Franklin Close**: Listing the pros and cons to help the prospect make a decision. This technique builds value by showing transparency and builds trust by allowing the prospect to see all sides of the decision.

10. **Puppy Dog Close**: Allowing the prospect to try the product before committing (e.g., a free trial). It builds trust by showing confidence in the product's value and reduces the risk for the prospect.

11. **Feel-Felt-Found Close**: Sharing a story about someone else who felt the same way but found value in the product. It builds trust by relating to the prospect's concerns and demonstrating how others have benefited.

12. **Scarcity Close**: Highlighting the limited availability of the product (e.g., "We only have a few left in stock"). This technique builds urgency and value while fostering trust through honest communication about availability.

13. **Takeaway Close**: Suggesting the prospect might not need the product, then emphasizing its value when they express interest. This technique builds trust by making the prospect feel their needs are being genuinely considered.

14. **Summary of Benefits Close**: Reiterating the specific benefits the prospect will receive. It builds value by reinforcing how

the product meets their needs and builds trust through clear, benefit-focused communication.

15. **Question Close**: Asking a question that assumes the prospect's interest (e.g., "How soon would you like to start using this product?"). It builds trust by engaging the prospect in envisioning their future with the product.

16. **Post-Purchase Behavior Close**: Asking about what happens after the sale to align with the prospect's goals (e.g., "How will this solution fit into your overall strategy?"). It builds trust by focusing on long-term value and integration.

17. **Solution Close**: Emphasizing how the product solves the prospect's specific problem (e.g., "This solution addresses all your concerns about X"). It builds value by directly linking the product to the prospect's needs.

18. **Accountability Close**: Asking the prospect to commit to a specific action or next step (e.g., "Can we schedule the installation for next week?"). This builds trust by creating a clear path forward and showing commitment to their needs.

19. **Visual Close**: Using visual aids or demonstrations to show the product in action. It builds value by providing a tangible sense of the product's benefits and fosters trust through concrete evidence.

20. **Reciprocity Close**: Offering a small concession or bonus to encourage the prospect to buy (e.g., "If you sign today, I can include a free accessory"). This builds value by adding extra benefit and trust by demonstrating goodwill and flexibility.

www.ingramcontent.com/pod-product-compliance
Lightning Source LLC
Chambersburg PA
CBHW071942120726
48001CB00005B/2001